D1052981

THEY DIED TOO YOUNG

DIANA, PRINCESS OF WALES

Vicki Cox

CHELSEA HOUSE PUBLISHERS
Philadelphia

The Chelsea House World Wide Web address is
http://www.chelseahouse.com

Printed and bound in The Hashemite Kingdom of Jordan.
First Printing
1 3 5 7 9 8 6 4 2

Cover photo: Princess Diana at the United Cerebral Palsy's annual
dinner at the New York Hilton, December 1995 (AP Photo)

Library of Congress Cataloging-in-Publication Data
Cox, Vicki.
    Diana, Princess of Wales / by Vicki Cox
        p. cm. — (They died too young.)
        Including bibliographical references.
        Summary: Discusses the life, marriage, and tragic death of Diana,
Princess of Wales.
        ISBN 0-7910-5854-9
        1. Diana, Princess of Wales—Juvenile literature. 2. Princess—
Great Britain—Biography—Juvenile literature. [1. Diana, Princess of
Wales, 1961–1997   2. Princesses.   3. Women—Biography.]
    I. Title. II. Series.
    DA591.A45 D5312 2000
    941.085'092—dc21
    [B]   00-026847
                                                     CIP

Picture Credits: AP Photo: pp. 4, 9, 10, 14, 16, 18, 23, 26, 32,
35, 38, 41, 44, 45

Publishing Coordinator Jim McAvoy
Editorial Assistant Rob Quinn
Contributing Editor Amy Handy

ABOUT THE AUTHOR

Vicki Cox writes freelance features for newspapers and
magazines in 16 states. Her anthology of features, *Rising
Stars and Ozark Constellations,* will be published in 2000.
Miss Cox has an M.S. in education and has taught for 25
years. She presently teaches sixth grade Social Studies at
Wood Middle School, Fort Leonard Wood, Missouri.

CONTENTS

Lady Diana Spencer marries Britain's Prince Charles on
July 29, 1981, in St. Paul's Cathedral.

HER ROYAL HIGHNESS

"Do I really have to go out there in front of all those people?" Lady Diana Spencer asked as she watched her wedding celebrations on television. People everywhere waited to see her beautiful blue eyes and radiant smile. They waited for a joyous bride in an enchanting white dress and shimmering veil. They waited for the next queen of England. She did indeed need to step outside and meet her future on July 29, 1981.

The hairdresser styled her blonde hair around a diamond tiara. The dress designers sewed the last stitch into her wedding gown. Her future grandmother-in-law, the Queen Mother, told her, "My dear, you look simply enchanting."

As she walked down the staircase at Clarence House, the Queen Mother's residence, her father, John Earl Spencer, exclaimed, "Darling, I'm so proud of you."

At exactly 10:30 A.M. she settled into the Glass Coach. Excitement overcame her nervousness, and she sang a few measures of a television ice cream commercial, "Just one Cornetto." With her wedding dress billowing against the red leather seat, Diana and her father rode to meet Prince Charles, the next king of England, Scotland, Wales, and Northern Ireland. Pulled by dapple-gray mares, the Glass Coach traveled through historic London streets to St. Paul's Cathedral, watched by 600,000 spectators lining the two-mile route. They waved from office buildings and apartment windows. They lifted their children high in the air to see her. They cheered and sang "Rule, Britannia" and "God Save the Queen."

Goodwill came from young and old. "Before, the Royal Family was something your parents were interested in," said an 18-year-old who had camped three days along the wedding route. "But Lady Diana seems so natural and young."

"It's a great day to be British," said a 72-year-old man who waited at the same place he'd been the night Prince Charles was born. "And now, here he is, about to be married. I say God bless him and her and all of us."

At the cathedral, a footman in scarlet opened the coach. When Diana emerged, the crowds gasped. She looked like a princess from a fairy tale.

Her ivory silk-taffeta dress was covered with pearls, lace, and bows. Its design included the traditional "something old, something new, something borrowed, something blue." The "old" was lace from Queen Mary, Prince Charles's great-grandmother. The "new" was thread British silkworms had spun for the dress. The "blue" was a small bow on the waistband. Diana "borrowed" her mother's diamond earrings. A tiny gold-and-diamond horseshoe symbolized good luck. The 25-foot train was the longest ever worn for an English wedding.

As her bridesmaids smoothed her dress and arranged her train, she jokingly asked, "Is he here yet?" Then she and her father climbed 24 steps to St. Paul's door. Another three-and-a-half minutes down the center of the cathedral waited her husband-to-be.

"I remember being so in love with my husband that I couldn't take my eyes off him," Diana later recalled. "I just absolutely thought I was the luckiest girl in the world."

Lucky? Three hundred thirty feet away waited both great wealth and luxury and lifelong responsibilities as the Princess of Wales, and the worries she carried in her heart were nearly as long. First, she had to help her father—handicapped from a stroke—make the long walk with her. Awaiting her were 2,500 guests. But among the world leaders, family, friends, and household staff, she searched for one particular person: Camilla Parker-Bowles. Diana worried that Prince Charles might still love his old girlfriend. Just two days before, he had given Camilla a gold bracelet. Diana worried about curtsying to Queen Elizabeth II, her new mother-in-law. Though her breakfast this day had stayed down, she had vomited everything the night before—a symptom of an eating disorder.

Lucky? During her engagement, Diana had innocently posed for photos as the sun shone through her skirt and silhouetted her legs. Once, she had worn a black strapless dress to a movie premier. Both incidents made headlines. Yet this Wednesday morning, kings, queens, and dignitaries waited for her. Their eyes glued to television sets in 70 countries, 750 million people watched her. Lip readers studied her, hoping to discover private words she might utter. Any mistake would be disastrous.

The trumpeters in the balcony and the cathedral organ played "Trumpet Voluntary," as she and her father walked slowly down the red carpet.

Afterward she admitted, "I was so nervous I hardly knew what I was doing." Eleven clergymen, five bridesmaids, and two page boys preceded her. When they parted, she saw Prince Charles, wearing his uniform as Commander of the Royal Navy. With gold braid and blue sash, he was dashing.

"You look wonderful," whispered Prince Charles as she arrived at the front of the church. "Wonderful for you," she said. The ceremony began.

"Here is the stuff of which fairy tales are made," said the Archbishop of Canterbury. The choir and organ performed an anthem specially commissioned by Prince Charles. Two other famous choirs sang. Diana's favorite hymn, "I Vow to Thee, My Country," ended the ceremony.

During the ceremony, both Diana and Prince Charles made small errors. Diana turned around Charles's names, calling him "Philip Charles Arthur George." Prince Charles's tongue tangled over whose money they would share—his or hers.

Within 70 minutes, the former kindergarten assistant, England's adopted Cinderella, was married to her charming prince. Though they did not kiss, Charles did whisper, "Well done" to his new wife. Diana curtsied perfectly for the queen. They signed wedding register No. 345, showing that "Charles P." and "Diana Spencer, spinster" had married. The couple stepped outside to greet the crowd. "Big Tom" and "Big Paul," the cathedral's largest bells, pealed from the northwest tower.

"Got out [of St. Paul's], was a wonderful feeling, everybody hurrahing, everybody happy because they thought we were happy and there was the big question mark in my mind," recalled Diana. "I realized I had taken on an enormous role but had no idea what I was going into."

The newlyweds rode to Buckingham Palace in an open carriage. Spectators waved flags and threw confetti. Gigantic photographs of Charles and Diana hung from a hotel. Rose petals showered down on them and a thousand doves were released. Princess Diana and Prince Charles smiled and waved.

At 1:15 P.M. the royals appeared on the balcony. Crowds yelled, "We want Di" over and over. The royal couple waved, left the balcony, and returned twice. "Kiss her, kiss her," the crowd yelled. Prince Charles resisted. "I'm not going in for that caper. They want us to kiss," he said. Diana reportedly answered, "Why ever not?" When they kissed, the crowds cheered louder. "It was just wonderful," said Diana.

"Neither of us will ever forget the atmosphere," the Prince later recalled. "It was electric, almost unbelievable. . . . I was quite extraordinarily proud to be British."

Inside Buckingham Palace, they posed for pictures and ate a champagne brunch with 118 family members. Charles cut the four-and-a-half-foot-tall wedding cake with a sword. The newlyweds were so busy they hardly had time to speak.

At 4:20 P.M., Princess Diana and Prince Charles left for the Waterloo Train station. He had changed from his uniform to a gray suit. Princess Diana wore a bright tangerine outfit and matching hat. Rose petals stuck to her dress. On the back of the carriage, Charles's brothers, Andrew and Edward, had attached a dozen balloons and a "Just Married" sign.

They Died Too Young

Prince Charles kisses his bride on the balcony of Buckingham Palace in London after their wedding.

Just before boarding the private train for her honeymoon, the new Princess of Wales surprised her wedding day organizer by kissing him impulsively on the cheek. Royal for just half a day, Diana was already reaching beyond the rules of protocol to touch people's lives. It was only the beginning.

England turned July 29, 1981, into a national holiday, celebrating with 10,000 parties. Some dressed as history's princes and princesses; others came as famous Charleses or Dianas. The royal family partied with First Lady Nancy Reagan and Princess Grace of Monaco until 4 A.M. Even Queen Elizabeth danced.

Briefly, people forgot life's ugly events. In 1981 both Pope John Paul II and President Ronald Reagan had been shot. The world laid aside racial problems and anxiety about joblessness to watch Diana and Charles marry. The sick, the poor, and the unhappy temporarily escaped their troubles by celebrating the "wedding of the century." English citizens felt close to their monarchy.

Everyone thought the royal couple would live happily ever after. They thought they could just peek in, like they had peered into Diana's glass carriage, anytime they wanted. After all, wasn't Diana the perfect Cinderella?

Nobody knew that Lady Diana wasn't really a storybook princess. She was just like everybody else, struggling with her own heartaches and problems. The glass slipper of a fairy-tale character never really fit.

DIANA, PRINCESS OF WALES   9

A family album picture shows Diana in her baby carriage
at Park House, Sandringham, Norfolk, in 1962.

THE HONORABLE
DIANA FRANCES SPENCER

Diana's childhood looked picture perfect. Family albums capture Diana smiling beside her brother Charles's baby buggy or diving into the family pool. She grins at the camera as her Shetland pony nuzzles her face, and she poses en pointe in ballet attire. Diana looked on top of the world. But she didn't always feel that way. Just getting born had its problems.

"I was the girl who was supposed to be a boy," she once said. The Spencers needed a male heir. Without a son, the title earl of Spencer, with its wealth and property, couldn't pass to Diana's father, John "Johnnie" Spencer, the Viscount Althorp. He needed a son to take his title before he could take a new one.

After the birth of Sarah and Jane in 1955 and 1957 respectively, baby John lived only 10 hours. Diana's parents wanted a son so much they chose no female names before their third daughter was born, on July 1, 1961.

The Honorable Diana Frances Spencer, all 7 pounds, 12 ounces of her, got her name a week later—"Diana" from an ancient ancestor and "Frances" from her mother, Frances Spencer. She was christened without fanfare in a Sandringham church. Her godparents were well-to-do-commoners. Diana sometimes felt her birth disappointed her parents and that if baby John had survived, she wouldn't have been born at all.

Diana's family lived at Park House on the queen's Sandringham Estates. Built by King Edward VII for royal guests, it was eventually leased to Diana's grandparents. Later, Lady Fermoy (Diana's maternal grandmother) gave it to Diana's parents as a wedding present.

Diana slept in a first-floor nursery and ate her meals with a nanny. Her mother's former governess came to Park House each day to tutor four-year-old Diana and several preschoolers. Diana learned from textbooks, and she learned aristocratic behavior.

Diana was a busy child. She loved to help take care of her little brother Charles. She sometimes slid down the staircase on a metal tray and hid the crusts of her tea sandwiches instead of eating them. Her menagerie of small pets included hamsters, rabbits, and Marmalade, a cat.

When Diana was six, people she loved started leaving her. Just when she was old enough to join her sisters in their downstairs classroom, they left for boarding school. Her governess and nanny left too.

In September 1967, the bottom fell out of Diana's world. Her mother left her father, taking Charles and Diana with her. The children saw their father only on weekends, but when the trio returned to Park House for Christmas, he wouldn't allow the children to leave. Their mother returned to London alone.

Today, the Spencers' breakup would hardly be noticed. But during the 1960s, it caused a scandal. People so near the royal court didn't air their private problems in public. When the wife of Frances's paramour, Peter Shand-Kidd, sued for divorce in April 1968, Frances was labeled an adulteress. Diana's father asked for custody of the children, and Frances's mother testified for him.

Diana was tugged between her parents. She worried about leaving her father when she visited her mother in London. She worried about leaving her mother when she returned to her father. She even worried when each parent gave her a pretty dress to wear to her cousin's wedding rehearsal. She didn't want to favor one parent over the other.

The Spencer divorce was final in 1969. Her father tried to be a good parent to Diana and Charles. He came into the playroom at teatime, asked about their pets, and even rented a camel for Diana's seventh birthday party. Because he was busy managing Park House estates and attending government or charity meetings, he hired a steady stream of nannies for Diana and Charles. The Spencer children were terrors, sticking pins in the women's chairs and throwing their clothes out the windows.

"It was a very unhappy childhood," Diana said. "Parents were busy sorting themselves out. Always seeing my mother crying. Daddy never spoke to us about it. We never asked questions . . . being very detached from everybody else."

People were surprised when Diana later revealed these feelings. Home movies and photos captured a bashful but smiling little girl. Household staff remember her scurrying about, helping her father. She made Charles straighten up his room. When Sarah visited from school, the future Princess of Wales dashed about washing her sister's clothes, making her bed, and running her bath.

During the day, Diana and Charles attended Sillfield School seven miles away. She and her 15 classmates learned lessons by repetition and practiced good manners. She dedicated her artwork to "Mummy and Daddy," but she didn't talk about them. Diana was the only girl at the school whose parents were divorced.

"The divorce helped me to relate to anyone else who is upset in their family life, whether it be stepfather syndrome or mother or whatever. I understand it," Diana later said.

From 1970 to 1973, Diana attended Riddlesworth Hall, two hours from Park House. She took her guinea pig, Peanuts, and a green hippo from her stuffed animal collection. Its painted luminescent eyes helped when she was afraid of the dark.

Despite her reluctance at being there, she settled into the school's routine. Instead of the spacious 10-bedroom Park

Another family photo shows Diana in Itchenor, West Sussex, during the summer of 1970.

House, she lived in a dormitory with a hundred girls. A cowbell woke them at 7:30 A.M. After breakfast, the girls said prayers, fed pets, and chanted their multiplication tables aloud.

Her parents came to visit on alternate weekends. She wrote them notes, asking for chocolate cake and ginger biscuits. Sweets were limited to one piece of candy a day during the week. Diana saved hers to gorge on weekends.

Riddlesworth offered new experiences for Diana. She loved the costumes and makeup of school plays. But the girl who later stood in the spotlight wanted only nonspeaking parts. She kept Peanuts's cage spotless and scolded those who didn't do the same for their pets. She worked hard at ballet, tennis, swimming, and diving. She made friends. At the end of her first year, she had earned the Legett Cup, a service award for helpfulness.

Diana's teachers thought she was pleasant but needed to be more studious. She knew her sisters and brother were better students. Once she sent her father a news clipping about successful people who had done poorly in school.

Twelve-year-old Diana left Riddlesworth for West Heath, the boarding school her mother and sisters had attended. They were hard acts to follow. Diana's mother had been captain of several teams and good enough at tennis for the Junior Wimbledon. Sarah was an excellent equestrienne, pianist, and actress. She passed six "O" (ordinary) levels— achievement tests necessary for Britain's General Certificate of Education. Jane was captain of the lacrosse team and had passed 11 O levels. Diana would never pass even one, essentially failing high school.

"It wasn't that she was stupid," a friend said. "Anyone who knows Diana knows how quick-witted she is. But she had this emotional hunger for passion and romance, for being wanted and needed, and didn't give a stuff about passing exams."

Diana liked stuffing herself, though. Breakfast included three or four helpings of cereal and all the baked beans on the table.

Diana in the Western Isles, Scotland, in 1974.

"I ate and ate and ate. It was always a great joke—let's get Diana to have three kippers [smoked fish] at breakfast and six pieces of bread, and I did all that."

Diana developed her own interests. She loved ballet, sneaking out of bed at night to practice. Though good at netball, lacrosse, and piano, she was outstanding at swimming and diving. Her "Spencer Special" dive didn't make a ripple.

Community work was another area in which Diana excelled. She helped an elderly lady in Sevenoaks every week, making tea, doing grocery shopping, and cleaning for her. Diana also played with disabled children at a nearby mental hospital. Connecting with the patients made her feel good about herself.

Once, after recovering from the flu, she returned to the infirmary to help serve meals to the girls. Such thoughtfulness earned her the Miss Clark Lawrence Award, another honor for service.

In 1975 her paternal grandfather died. He had been an unpleasant man who favored his art collection over his wife and only son. Diana's father inherited Althorp's 13,000 acres and became the eighth Earl Spencer. Charles became the Viscount Althorp and his sisters became "Ladies." Spencers had been living at Althorp in Northamptonshire for 500 years. Its 121 rooms were decorated with tapestries and antique furniture. Art experts admired its paintings, books, and silver collections.

They Died Too Young

In 1977 her father remarried, without inviting his children to the ceremony. He and Raine McCorquodale had fallen in love working on a book; she wrote the text for his photographs. A formidable woman, well-known in local government, Raine divorced her husband of 28 years, and took both Johnnie and his house by storm.

With Althorp came huge inheritance taxes and yearly operating expenses. To generate some income, Raine remodeled the house and opened a gift shop and a tea room for tourists. To finance her redecorating, she sold off more than 300 prized masterpieces.

But the iron hand that saved the family from financial ruin couldn't touch the children with tenderness. To them, Raine was a loud, overdressed stepmother. Sarah gave orders to the servants over her head. Jane didn't speak to Raine for two years. Charles tried to push her fully clothed into the pool, and Diana wanted a friend to write a poison-pen letter. They avoided her whenever possible.

Diana failed her O levels both in June and December 1977. "I just remember thinking that I wasn't very good at anything, that I was hopeless," Diana recalled.

Her father sent her to Switzerland to study French, cooking, and sewing. But she liked skiing and laughing with friends more than schoolwork. She convinced her parents that she was wasting their money and should come home.

Lady Diana Frances Spencer had no place to go. She tiptoed around her parents' lives with their new spouses. A high school "dropout," ineligible for university studies, she lacked marketable skills. She was too tall for her real love, the ballet. Working with children or the handicapped was possible, but she had no real direction.

Lady Diana Spencer in July 1981.

SHY DI

Returning from Switzerland in March 1978, Diana wanted to live in London. But her parents found a job for the 16-year-old cleaning, cooking, and babysitting for friends. After Diana's pleas, her parents agreed she could use her mother's Chelsea apartment. She worked for temporary employment agencies as a waitress for private parties and as a cleaning lady.

In September, Diana's father suffered a cerebral hemorrhage. He was in a coma for months. His wife literally saved his life, talking to him constantly and obtaining new medications for him. Raine and his children quarreled bitterly about their visits. Sympathetic nurses permitted Diana and her brother to slip in when Raine wasn't there.

As her father recovered, Diana worked for the Vacani School of Dance, supervising two dozen toddlers, but she soon quit because she had hurt her ankle skiing in the French Alps. During the holiday that included pillow fights and practical jokes, she told a friend, "It would be nice if I could be a dancer—or 'the Princess of Wales.'"

Diana moved into her own apartment after her 18th birthday. Everyone agreed about her good times at 60 Coleherne Court. "I laughed my head off there. . . . [I] loved being on my own," she remembered.

She redecorated the sitting room in yellow and the bathroom in red cherries. She put "Chief Chick" on her bedroom door and organized cleaning schedules for the three-bedroom flat.

Diana and her roommates acted like girls at summer

camp. They phoned people with unusual names late at night and put sticky tape on friends' car locks. After James Gilbey canceled a date, Diana smeared eggs and flour over his car. Diana neither smoked nor drank, but she liked preparing dinner parties. Between courses she would jump up to wash dirty dishes.

She didn't have many boyfriends. "I'd always kept them away, thought they were all trouble—and I couldn't handle it emotionally. I was very screwed up." She also secretly believed in an important destiny. "I knew somehow that I had to keep myself very tidy for whatever was coming my way."

The "whatever" was someone royal. The Spencers knew the royal children, who swam in the Spencers' heated swimming pool. They attended birthday parties together. Prince Charles was dating Diana's sister, Sarah, in November 1977 when Sarah organized a hunting party at Althorp, inviting Diana.

Charles remembered a "very jolly and amusing and attractive 16-year-old—full of fun." Diana recalled, "I remember being a fat, podgy, no make-up, unsmart lady but I made a lot of noise, and he liked that."

But nothing romantic developed then or when she attended the Prince's 30th birthday party. Their destinies overlapped two years later at a July barbecue. Sitting together on a hay bale, they talked about the televised funeral of Charles's uncle. "You looked so sad." Diana told him. "My heart bled for you when I watched. I thought: 'It's wrong, you're lonely, you should be with somebody to look after you.'" Charles appreciated her kindness.

The Prince of Wales needed a wife, one who would one day be queen of England. The ideal candidate was a Protestant virgin. So he dated British aristocrats and beautiful blondes. In 1971 Charles found his own true love—daring, witty, outdoorsy Camilla Shand. But Charles didn't act quickly enough, and she married Andrew Parker-Bowles. The other women weren't quite right. Either they had already had love affairs, or they made foolish mistakes with the press.

Diana was too young to have a past, and she had a very British pedigree—her relatives had prestigious jobs with royalty. Her grandmothers had attended the Queen Mother as ladies-in-waiting. Diana's father had been an equerry (a private secretary) to Charles's mother and grandfather. Diana's ancestors were distantly connected to two kings. "I'm beginning to think she is more Royal than I am," Charles joked.

After their hay bale conversation, Diana was invited to the royal family's estates. When she turned up on their yacht in August, Charles saw Diana in a different light. He sent red roses to her and invited her to Balmoral, his family's Scotland retreat. She did everything he did, stalking deer and fishing.

Journalist James Whitaker of the *Daily Star,* who routinely watched the royals through binoculars, first glimpsed Diana behind a tree, spying on him with the mirror in her compact. He admired her inventiveness. He phoned in the story of Charles's new girlfriend. Rival tabloid the *Sun*'s September 8 headline trumpeted, *"HE'S IN LOVE AGAIN! DI IS THE NEW GIRL FOR CHARLES."*

In truth, they were really just beginning to be friends. But the press had already fallen in love with Diana, enchanted by her creamy complexion, blue eyes, and sweet smile. Since she had a habit of hanging her head to minimize her height, the press nicknamed her "Shy Di." Reporters waited outside her apartment, telephoned her at all hours, and even stalked her into a department store's lingerie department. One even tried to climb through the window of Young England Kindergarten to watch her at work.

By 1979 she was a teaching assistant, helping children play, teaching them dance, changing diapers, and comforting them when they cried. One mother remembered, "She was really wonderful with the little ones. She had a real empathy with them."

To stop the press from bothering the children, she agreed

to pose once with her students. Photographers positioned them so the sunlight shone through her sheer skirt, outlining her figure. She wept in embarrassment.

"Everywhere I go, there is someone there," she complained. "If I go to the restaurant or just out shopping in the supermarket, they're trying to take photographs. . . . It's just not right at all."

To meet Charles, she drove to her sister's or a friend's apartment and sneaked out the back into a car driven by Charles's valet. Her roommates sometimes drove her car, luring away the press so Diana could leave unseen. Once she even escaped out her kitchen window by climbing down some knotted sheets.

Diana eventually asked for protection. Though the royals despised her predicament, they wouldn't help her unless Charles proposed marriage. Everyone pressured Charles to propose. The press loved Diana. His family liked her. The people adored her. Even Camilla Parker-Bowles approved. Still, Charles seemed merely fond of Diana.

She, on the other hand, was head over heels in love with the prince. If he fished, Diana, the city girl, quietly watched him. If he read philosophy, the bubblegum kid listened patiently. While he hunted, she waited, needlepointing with the Queen Mother.

Considering the future, Charles invited Diana to Camilla's for the weekend. "If I were to ask you [to marry me], do you think it would be possible?" he asked. The Big Question came a year later. When he officially proposed, on February 6, she joked, "Yeah, OK." Then she quit giggling and said, "Yes, please." Later she recalled something told to her: "You won't be Queen, but you'll have a tough role."

When she told her roommates, she recalled, "Everybody screamed and howled, and we went for a drive around London with our secret."

Two days later, she visited her mother in Australia to rest and to make plans. When Diana returned, the queen announced their engagement on February 24. "I'm amazed that she's even brave enough to take me on," Charles said in a television interview.

"And I suppose in love?" asked a reporter.

Diana immediately responded, "Of course." The prince, however, hesitated, "Whatever 'in love' means."

But Diana's 18-carat sapphire engagement ring enclosed her in a new life. She moved behind royal walls, with a bodyguard assigned to her. As she left her apartment, he warned, "This is the last night of freedom in your life, so make the most of it."

Prince Charles and Lady Diana at Buckingham Palace after announcing their engagement on February 24, 1981.

She stayed with the Queen Mother but soon secretly settled into a suite near Charles in Buckingham Palace. She learned how to enter and exit a room, wave, curtsy, and sign official papers. But the 19-year-old quickly realized there was more to being a princess. She was overwhelmed by her advisors' briefings. When left on her own, instead of studying information, she tap-danced in the music room or wandered the massive halls plugged into her Walkman. The prince never changed his appointments to be with her, something she didn't understand.

"[T]hen the tears started," said her former roommate. "She wasn't happy. She was suddenly plunged into all this pressure."

Something worse than loneliness awaited her. Diana believed her long struggle with bulimia began when Charles touched her waistline and teased, "Oh, a bit chubby here, aren't we?" A month later, Diana chose a strapless black dress for her first royal appearance. She didn't know that royals wore black only for mourning and never wore revealing dresses. Diana was mortified by the commotion her dress caused when she left the car. Later she confided her embarrassment to Princess Grace of Monaco.

"Don't worry," Princess Grace said, "it will get a lot worse."

It did. The headlines and descriptions of her "puppy fat" pushed Diana closer to bulimia nervosa. People with this problem gorge their food and then purposefully vomit or purge by overusing laxatives. Anxious, insecure women (and sometimes even men) with troubled childhoods can develop bulimia. Diana was a perfect candidate.

"You inflict it upon yourself because your self-esteem is at a low ebb," she said. "You fill your stomach up four or five times a day . . . it gives you a feeling of comfort. It's like having a pair of arms around you, but it's temporary. Then you're disgusted at the bloatedness of your stomach and then you bring it all up again."

Diana feared her royal responsibilities and Charles's lack of attention. His former girlfriend, Camilla, lurked nearby, inviting Diana to lunch before Diana even knew her own schedule and telephoning Charles as he left for a tour of India.

The gold bracelet Diana discovered in Charles's office five days before the wedding fueled her suspicions. Its engraved initials symbolized "Gladys" and "Fred," Camilla's and Charles's nicknames for each other. Diana didn't want Charles to give Camilla the bracelet, but the prince insisted. Three days later, he delivered his present while Diana confessed to her sisters, "I can't marry him, I can't do this, this is absolutely unbelievable." But they all made light of it, saying, "Your face is on the tea-towels so you're too late to chicken out."

They Died Too Young

Diana's inner despair became obvious. She broke into tears at Charles's polo match just days before the wedding. At the final wedding rehearsal she publicly cried again. The press wondered if she was ready for her new royal role.

But the country's celebrations had begun. The night before the wedding, Charles lit a chain of bonfires that spread across England. The country's biggest fireworks display ever lit the sky over Hyde Park. Charles watched from Buckingham Palace. Diana spent the night "sick as a parrot," bingeing and purging.

"The day I walked down the aisle at St. Paul's Cathedral, I felt that my personality was taken away from me, and I was taken over by the royal machine," she recalled.

It should have been the happiest day of her life.

Prince Charles and Princess Diana leave St. Mary's
Hospital with Prince Henry ("Harry") in September 1984.

MRS. CHARLES WINDSOR
AND MUMMY

Mrs. Charles Windsor quickly learned what life was going to be like as a royal. She wanted to curl up with Charles on their honeymoon. Charles, 13 years older, wanted to curl up with a stack of books. Diana wanted her new husband completely to herself. But dinners on the royal yacht, *Britannia,* were formal affairs with the ship's uniformed officers. Diana wanted Charles's past to disappear. Instead, she found photographs of Camilla in his engagement calendar and discovered a pair of gold cuff links she had given him.

Charles was learning too. Diana could happily picnic on a sandy beach or fly into a jealous rage. She could playfully plop into his lap or abruptly burst into tears. Growing up with quietly controlled and distant emotions, he was unprepared for her unpredictable moods. As a toddler, he saw his mother only 30 minutes a day. Imitating the soldiers who attended her ceremonial duties, he once saluted instead of hugging her. Diana's needs were loud and messy. From the beginning, neither understood the other.

In Alexandria, Diana and Charles invited Egyptian President Anwar al-Sadat and his wife aboard the *Britannia.* Nervous about entertaining as "Her Royal Highness" for the first time, Diana babbled on about loving tropical fruits like mangoes. Forgetting diplomatic behavior, she affectionately kissed her important guests good-bye, surprising them and embarrassing Charles.

When she was alone, Diana's bulimia worsened. She threw up four or five times a day, even as she consumed bowls of ice cream and snacks between meals. "Anything I could find I would gobble up and be sick two minutes later," she remembered.

After returning to Balmoral, the quarreling between Charles and Diana intensified. Shouting and arguing, Diana tried to force him to pay attention to her. She cried for hours, head in hands. He didn't understand her dramatics.

In his own way, Charles tried. He asked his favorite South African philosopher to talk with her. Then he sent her to London psychiatrists, who prescribed tranquilizers.

Her in-laws could not relate to her problems. They never commended her for a job well done because that was something they expected of themselves and their fellow royals. They didn't think she was ill because they were never ill themselves. They didn't understand her outbursts because they never showed their feelings. And because they kept their distance, Diana cried and binged and purged even more. She weighed only 110 pounds.

Then she learned she was pregnant. That ended the doctors' campaign of sedatives. At last she was doing something right, having a baby for the throne of England. The bad news was the side effects. If she wasn't in the bathroom forcing herself to vomit, she was vomiting with morning sickness.

When she wasn't sick, she redecorated their two homes, one in Highgrove, a country estate near the Parker-Bowleses; the other was a 25-room apartment at Kensington Palace.

The 20-year-old met herself coming and going. Her photo filled newsstands. She thought the world's interest in her would eventually disappear, but the Diana magic just kept growing.

In October, before her pregnancy was announced, she began her first official tour, a three-day "walkabout" through Wales. She was terrified of the crowds and of making speeches. Between appearances, she cried uncontrollably.

They Died Too Young

But when the car stopped, she walked right into the crowds, smiling and laughing. No one suspected she was so afraid.

The people of Wales noticed her special touch. She dressed in red, white, and green, their national colors. She didn't wear gloves, so women could see her rings. She thanked spectators for waiting in the cold and rain. When a seven-year-old boy yelled, "My dad says give us a kiss," she replied, "Well then, you better have one." A royal kissing a commoner? The crowds cheered.

Diana was a triumph. Charles carried her flowers and apologized that he didn't have enough wives to work both sides of the street. At tour's end she was given the Freedom of the City of Cardiff award. Her acceptance speech included a sentence in Welsh. People loved it—and her.

She tried to do her job correctly. Because she refused nausea medication, she sometimes ran out of state dinners to be sick. Instead of going to bed to rest, she'd return to finish out the evening. "I felt it was my duty to sit at the table," she said.

In private, she and Charles argued loud and long. "Shy Di" ranted and raved. Her desperate cries for help, disguised in angry words, went unheeded. In January 1982, as Charles left to go riding, Diana threw herself down the stairs. (This was not the only time she purposefully hurt herself for his benefit.) Though four months pregnant, she was only bruised around the stomach, and the unborn child was not harmed.

On June 21, 1982, at 9:03 P.M., England gave her its undivided attention. With Charles helping, Diana delivered a 7-pound, 1½-ounce boy. The crowd of 500 outside the hospital cheered. Theater audiences stood and applauded. For a week, the future king of England was simply "Baby Wales." Then his parents finally agreed on his name, William Arthur Philip Louis.

Diana loved baby William, but instead of being deliriously happy, she was hit with postpartum depression, a temporary condition new mothers sometime experience. She avoided solo public appearances, venturing out only to light the Christmas lights on Regent Street in London and to attend Princess Grace's funeral in Monaco in 1982.

Diana's private terrors caused several alarming incidents during the autumn of 1982. Still fearing that Charles loved Camilla, she wanted his comfort and reassurance. On separate occasions, she slashed her wrists with a razor, cut her thighs and chest with a pen knife, and threw herself into a glass display at Kensington Palace. Her violence drove him further away.

Rumors of their arguments were interesting the press. Newspapers really perked up when Diana publicly angered the royal family. Refusing to accompany Charles to an important ceremony, she eventually showed up late. The queen was insulted. Charles looked foolish for explaining she was ill. The media wondered if the marriage had soured or if Diana was about to have a nervous breakdown. Diana, who always read the articles, felt the press's criticism deeply.

"One minute I was nobody, the next minute I was Princess of Wales, mother, media toy, member of this family, you name it, and it was too much for one person at that time," she later explained. Little did she realize what was ahead for her.

In March 1983 the royal couple embarked on a six-week tour of Australia and New Zealand. They traveled 45,000 miles, shook more than 6,000 hands, and were photographed constantly. The 100,000 people who jammed into Brisbane's square nearly caused a riot. People were knocked to the ground. Children got lost. In the middle of it all was Diana, bravely smiling.

"The whole world was focusing on me every day," she said. "I thought that this was just so appalling, I hadn't done something specific like climb [Mt.] Everest or done something wonderful like that."

Though resentful of Diana's media attention, Charles constantly encouraged and complimented his wife. They fre-

They Died Too Young

quently smiled and touched each other. To relax, they traveled to the sheep ranch where William and his nanny were staying. They had brought the toddler on the trip at the Australian prime minister's invitation. It was the first time a child so young had joined royal parents on a foreign tour.

The Australian tour proved that Diana could perform as a British royal. She was even more than royal; she was a worldwide superstar. Though weak from her bulimia, she stood up to the tour's demands. Back in England, Diana and Charles appeared at charity affairs and became patrons of 12 organizations. Together they made 76 public engagements; Diana attended 45 more alone. Queen Elizabeth complimented her on her improvements.

But very unsettling rumors about a mismatch between Diana and Charles surfaced. He liked opera; she liked Elton John. He liked the quiet country; she preferred city lights. He enjoyed philosophy; she favored the "soaps." Friends who had been close to Charles became her enemies. Loyal staff members resigned or were fired. Diana was blamed.

Valentine's Day, 1984, was another day Diana could have celebrated. Charles and Diana announced that she was pregnant again. Both wanted a girl. But Diana knew from an ultrasound test that the child was another boy. She kept the news from her husband. Fourteen-pound Prince Henry Charles Albert David was born September 15, 1984.

A remark Charles made at the birth of Harry (as he was nicknamed) deeply affected Diana's feelings about her marriage. Whether Charles was genuinely disappointed or simply teasing her, Diana remembered him saying, "Oh God, it's a boy, and he's even got red hair." Diana later said of that moment, "Something inside me closed off."

Diana had provided an heir and a "spare" to the throne. She performed publicly as a responsible royal with a style and warmth people loved. She had done everything she was supposed to do as wife of the Prince of Wales. But rumors persisted. This was not a live-happily-ever-after fairy tale.

The Prince and Princess of Wales with their sons, Prince Harry and Prince William, in the Sicily Islands in June 1989.

THE PEOPLE'S PRINCESS

Diana was very unhappy. Her marriage was dissolving one argument at a time, and the media divulged her every twitch. In October 1985 the couple decided to speak on television about their public duties, rumors about their marriage, and Diana's health. Diana said her primary role was "supporting my husband whenever I can." She denied dieting, saying, "Maybe I'm so scrawny because I take so much exercise." Charles admitted to "becoming more eccentric as I get older."

The press cooed about their confident performance. "What a smashing royal couple they are," said the *Daily Mirror*. They gave the pair high marks for their Australian and American tours.

But at home, Diana and Charles led separate lives. She partied without him. He visited friends he had abandoned for her. Rather than argue, they communicated through notes. They traveled separately, even when going to the same place, often on different days. Diana was often reduced to tears because of it.

The palace denied reports that she was bulimic. But during the couple's 1986 tour of Japan and Canada, her eating problem couldn't be ignored. Visiting the Expo exhibit in Vancouver, Diana fainted. Having eaten only a chocolate bar over several days, she told Charles, "Darling, I think I'm about to disappear."

Charles' scolded her for not excusing herself when she felt ill yet insisted she appear as scheduled later that evening. He returned to the companionship of Camilla. When Diana found out, her bulimia went out of control. She slashed herself. Charles was unmoved. Diana then turned to

James Hewitt, a cavalry captain who was helping her overcome her fear of horses. Their affair lasted five years.

She developed her friendship with Sarah Ferguson. Diana had played matchmaker between Prince Andrew and "Fergie," whose mischievousness was a refreshing change from stuffy royal protocol. Together, they'd dressed as policewomen to crash Prince Andrew's bachelor party. At Ascot, a high-society event, they playfully poked a friend's backside with an umbrella. The press reported their antics, sometimes comparing Diana unfavorably to the high-spirited redhead.

Then a ski vacation tragedy in Switzerland helped restore Diana's positive press coverage and raised her self-esteem. Charles and two friends were caught in an avalanche. Hugh Lindsay was killed and the other friend was seriously injured. Charles was immobilized by grief. Diana jumped in, organizing the return of Lindsay's body to England and insisting they accompany it. The press praised her, and she liked herself better too.

A counselor helped Diana begin looking beyond her disappointing marriage. She realized that, by reaching out to others, she could make a real difference in the world. "I want to do what I can to help, to make life better for people, to relieve suffering and distress," she said. Charity organizers knew the Princess of Wales ensured long guest lists and large donations to their causes. Raising funds was important. But the people these charities helped received something more precious than money. They got Diana's smile and touch.

In April 1987 Diana shocked everyone by shaking hands with an AIDS patient without wearing protective clothing. People had believed AIDS was a gay man's disease, spread through intimate contact. They changed their minds when the glamorous Diana wasn't afraid to touch the ill.

She publicly supported the National AIDS Trust and similar organizations. Diana also stood by her friend Adrian Ward-Jackson, who was diagnosed with AIDS. She even brought Princes William and Harry with her when she visited hospices

They Died Too Young

and homeless shelters. "Am I doing them a favor if I hide suffering and unpleasantness from them until the last possible minute?" she asked.

While the press still photographed her in diamonds, the cameras also captured Diana with the people: Diana holding a leukemia-stricken toddler in her lap; Diana caressing an elderly person's cheek; Diana hugging children with AIDS. Her personal touch and her one-to-one conversations made each of them feel special.

Diana talks with AIDS patient Wayne Taylor at the Casey House AIDS hospice in Toronto in 1991.

Her schedule grew to 250 engagements, including Birthright, an organization supporting research for the unborn, and Turning Point, which assisted drug addicts, alcoholics, and the mentally ill. Diana chose causes that society chose to ignore until she wrapped her arms and her celebrity around them.

But nothing changed at home. Charles and Diana agreed to keep their troubles private by living secret, separate lives. He used Highgrove as his home, she used Kensington Palace as hers. They would appear in public together and try to act happy.

Diana's bulimia and her emotions were still out of control. Finally, she confessed her condition to her former roommate, Carolyn Bartholomew, who threatened to go to the press if

Diana didn't seek help. Diana phoned an eating disorders expert. Though she refused to be hospitalized, the therapy and books he gave her helped. While her bulimia continued through her life, her vomiting episodes diminished.

When Prince William was hurt in an accident at boarding school, Diana again became the press's darling. In June 1991 the prince was struck in the forehead with a golf club and required surgery to smooth out the bones. While the operation wasn't life-threatening, it wasn't just a simple procedure either. Diana stayed with William through the night. But Charles, reassured that William's injury wasn't serious, fulfilled his official duties by entertaining European officials at the opera and traveling to a conference on environmental issues. He visited William the next day. One report headlined Diana's behavior with "The Exhausted Face of a Loving Mother." Charles's dedication to duty earned quite another: "What Kind of Dad Are You?" asked the *Sun*.

In the past, royals had survived in unhappy marriages. The trick was in pretending to live happily ever after. But Charles and Diana's misery was hard to ignore. Diana celebrated her 30th birthday without Charles. She sent her own Christmas cards, signed, "Lots of love, Diana." On tour in India, she deliberately turned away from Charles's kiss and posed alone at the Taj Mahal, a shrine to love. When her father died of a heart attack, Diana and Charles arrived and departed the funeral separately.

Then, in June 1992, Andrew Morton's biography *Diana: Her True Story* exposed everything. Morton told editors, "Treat that book as though the Princess had signed every page."

Publicly she denied cooperating with Morton, though she had secretly answered his questions on tape. She hoped to reveal the Camilla-Charles affair and explain her depressions and bulimia. She received tremendous public support but angered the royal family—and her husband.

After excerpts from the book were printed, Charles and Diana agreed to an official separation. But before the legalities were announced, more secrets came out. In August the transcript of a telephone conversation revealed the relationship between Diana and another lover, James Gilbey.

In November the prince and princess traveled together to Seoul, Korea, trying to appear reconciled. But Diana's tears and Charles's discomfort were so tortured, the press dubbed them "The Glums."

Soon another telephone conversation made headlines. This time, Charles talked passionately to Camilla. Nobody could ignore the unpleasant truth. After Diana had prepared William and Harry, the decision was made public. On December 9, Prime Minister John Major officially announced the separation.

As Diana later said, "The fairy tale had come to an end." The announcement placed Diana in a never-never land. She wasn't divorced, and she wasn't a wife. She wasn't an official royal, and she wasn't a commoner. Still, the separation freed her to find herself and a more fulfilling role for the world's queen of hearts.

Mother Teresa meets with Princess Diana at the
Missionaries of Charity convent in the South Bronx
section of New York in 1997.

ENGLAND'S ROSE

If the fairy tale princess didn't exist, there were still plenty of other Dianas to go around: Diana the humanitarian, Diana the brave, Diana the mother.

Diana was a wonderful mother. Her joy in William (called Wills) and Harry was obvious. She showered them with affection. She took them to McDonald's and braved amusement park rides with them. She called them every day at school. She incorporated their activities into her busy schedule.

She was determined that her boys know the normal world outside the gilded circle of their crowns. She insisted they attend school with other children. She continued to take them with her to homeless shelters and hospices.

"I want them to have an understanding of people's emotions, people's insecurities, people's distress, and people's hopes and dreams," she said.

Diana the humanitarian supported 118 charities. Appearing about once every other day, she traveled from Nepal to Zimbabwe. She met with Calcutta's Mother Teresa. Once terrified of the microphone, she spoke out at Britain's first conference on eating disorders and at a conference on depression. In October she and Prime Minister John Major discussed her becoming a goodwill ambassador, an idea the royal family disliked.

But her schedule was impossibly full. At a luncheon for Headway National Head Injuries, she abruptly announced her retirement to a "meaningful public role with a more private life." She made just 10 royal appearances in 1994.

On June 29 a two-and-a-half-hour documentary showcased Charles's views on public service, the monarchy, politics, parenting, and the press. But one sentence made headlines when the interviewer asked if he had been faithful to his marriage. "Yes," Charles admitted, "until it became irretrievably broken down, us both having tried."

Diana didn't watch her husband admit he'd been cheating on her since 1986. Instead, she attended a fund-raising dinner at London's Serpentine Gallery. She bounded out of the car, smiling and flirtatious in a short, formfitting dress. From head to toe, Diana bravely seemed to scoff, "Do I care?"

In October, there was more. In a biography, Charles said he was pressured by the media to propose to Diana and that he had been uneasy about her moods. He admitted he felt Diana was "lovable" and "warm-hearted" and "was sure he could fall in love with her." No one knew how brokenhearted she was.

In 1995 Diana the humanitarian came out of retirement to travel to Japan, Russia, Argentina, Italy, France, and the United States. She attended fund-raisers for cancer, homeless shelters, drug rehabilitation centers, and leprosy.

Diana's vengeful side kept popping up. In 1994, the tabloids had reported the dozens of crank phone calls she made to Oliver Hoare, a married man. *Princess in Love,* James Hewitt's version of his secret relationship with Diana, hit the bookshelves soon after. In 1995 she was accused of taking up with rugby captain Will Carling.

Diana struck back. Talking on BBC-TV, she exposed more dirty business. She admitted loving Hewitt. She admitted "the Squidgy tapes" with Gilbey. She denied helping with the Morton biography. Politicians and the press were stunned. Her close friend Rosa Monckton said, "It was Diana at her worst."

Yet surprisingly, the public embraced the vengeful Diana. Some liked her even better. Others suggested she become an ambassador. Just after the November 20 interview, 6,000 unhappy women wrote her. Still, Diana paid for her spitefulness. A month later, Queen Elizabeth's handwritten letter arrived, "suggesting" that Charles and Diana divorce.

The divorce was finalized on August 28, 1996. Diana received a $27 million lump sum settlement, $600,000 yearly office and household expenses, and shared custody of her sons. No longer "Her Royal Highness," she was simply "Diana, Princess of Wales."

Diana's life took new directions in 1997. With January's four-day visit to Angola she wanted "to get her hands dirty" and "find a new level of seriousness," according to an observer. Viewing horrible photographs of land-mine victims, she asked, "Do you think I could make a difference?"

Diana watches a land-mine clearing in Huambo, central Angola, in January 1997.

Far away from her glittering world, she toured the country where one out of every 334 inhabitants was an amputee. Wearing flak jacket and visor, she walked through minefields and talked with victims whose hands, legs, or feet had been blown off. Because 60 journalists and a BBC film crew trailed her, the world saw how terrible the effects of land mines were.

Four months later, Britain's foreign secretary announced that Britain would destroy its stockpiled land mines and support a worldwide ban. Diana was among the "anti-mine campaigners" credited.

Diana shed more of her former life. The idea to sell her clothes for charity had been William's, and Diana liked it. Auctioned at Christie's in New York, her 79 dresses raised $3.26 million for the AIDS Crisis Trust and for the Cancer Research Fund for the Royal Maraden Hospital.

Diana the woman took the spotlight in July. She needed

to get away. Her two-year romance with a Pakistani heart surgeon ended, and Charles was busy planning Camilla's 50th birthday party at Highgrove. Mohamed al-Fayed, one of her father's acquaintances, invited her to southern France. The paparazzi snapped on their telephoto lenses as Diana, Wills, and Harry jet-skied and swam near the Egyptian's 190-foot yacht. Also aboard was Emad "Dodi" al-Fayed, her host's 42-year-old son. The press pounced on Dodi's reputation for unpaid bills, former cocaine addiction, and playboy romances. But Diana didn't seem to care—either about Dodi's past or the photographers watching them. She and Dodi looked happy.

Diana returned the boys to London July 20, promising to see them after they visited their father in Balmoral. It never happened. The next day she cuddled a four-year-old child with cancer, flew to Italy for the funeral of fashion designer Gianni Versace, and then joined Dodi on the Mediterranean.

Her land-mine tour of Bosnia began August 8. For three days she visited victims, villages, and cemeteries. The hundred journalists with her focused on her romance with Dodi.

After the Bosnia trip, she and Dodi happily cruised the Mediterranean again, and then flew to Paris. Nearly 50 paparazzi, on motorbikes and cars, followed them from Dodi's apartment, his father's estate, and his family's hotel. At the Ritz, Diana gave Dodi her father's treasured cuff links and a gold cigar clipper inscribed, "From Diana with love." Trailed by photographers, they drove to his apartment, a restaurant, and back to the Ritz on August 31. Then they decided to return to his apartment, where a fabulous ring and a poem engraved in silver awaited her. A decoy car left the front entrance while Dodi's Mercedes left from the back. Some photographers followed.

Driving through the Place de l'Alma tunnel at 85 miles per hour, their driver, Henri Paul, apparently swerved to avoid a slower car, hit the wall, and crashed into concrete dividing pillars. Dodi and Paul died instantly. A bodyguard was seriously injured. Diana, trapped in the wreckage, was barely alive.

The photographers arrived. Some snapped pictures. One, also a trained paramedic, tried to assist Diana, and a French doctor driving in the opposite lane stopped to help.

But Diana's chest was crushed. She lost a lot of blood from a large wound in her left pulmonary vein. After surgery and two hours of external and internal heart massage, physicians couldn't restore her circulation. On August 31, 1997, Diana, Princess of Wales, was pronounced dead.

At first the paparazzi were blamed. Ten photographers were charged with manslaughter and for violating a law requiring passersby to help accident victims. But the driver, Henri Paul, was responsible. Tests showed his blood-alcohol level was four times over legal limits. Also found were an antidepressant drug and medication for alcoholism that could have affected his judgment.

Prince Charles and Diana's two sisters brought Diana's body back to London. Mourners gathered in the city. Millions of bouquets piled waist deep against the palace walls. Children laid crayoned notes among the flowers. Others lit candles and wept at the gates and waited to sign books of condolences. But while shocked Britons reached out to each other in their grief, the queen stayed silent behind Balmoral's walls. The flag flew at full-mast over Buckingham Palace.

"Where is the Queen when the country needs her?" one newspaper asked.

The sadness of Diana's death finally united the monarchy and its subjects. The royal family returned to London. Prince Charles and his sons talked and shook hands with mourners. Finally, in a televised speech, Queen Elizabeth praised Diana.

"In good times and bad, she never lost her capacity to smile and laugh, nor to inspire others with her warmth and kindness," she said. "No one who knew Diana will ever forget her."

On September 6, 1997, Diana again brought the world together. Two million people lined the funeral route; three

At left, the Duke of Edinburgh, Prince William, Earl Spencer, Prince Harry, and Prince Charles join the funeral cortege of Diana, Princess of Wales, at Buckingham Palace, Saturday, September 6, 1997.

billion more watched on television. Draped in maroon and gold, her coffin journeyed to Westminster Abbey. Three white bouquets, lilies from the Spencers, tulips from William, and roses, with a card inscribed "Mummy" from Prince Harry, lay on top.

Diana's brother, Princes Harry and William, Charles, and Philip (Charles's father) followed her horse-drawn gun carriage as spectators wept. Behind them, 500 charity representatives, in wheelchairs and on crutches, followed. Queen Elizabeth, standing outside Buckingham Palace, bowed her head as the coffin passed. Her nod, and the lowering of Britain's flag, showed Diana great respect.

Inside Westminster Abbey, Diana's friends—including actor Tom Cruise, First Lady Hillary Rodham Clinton, and Althorp's cleaning lady—joined the royals. Diana's sister Sarah and England's prime minister read from a poem and the Bible. But the most eloquent words were Elton John's. Revising his "Candle in the Wind" lyrics he sang:

They Died Too Young

Seen here in an aerial view, Princess Diana is buried on the grounds of the Spencer family estate in Althorp, England, north of London.

Goodbye England's rose:
    may you ever grow in our hearts.
You were the grace that placed itself
    where lives were torn apart.
You called out to our country,
    and you whispered to those in pain
Now you belong to heaven,
    and the stars spell out your name.
And it seems to me you lived your life
    like a candle in the wind. . . .

Her brother's tribute was angry. He criticized the monarchy, declaring that Diana "needed no royal title to continue to generate her particular brand of magic." He attacked the press, noting that like Diana, the ancient Greek goddess of the hunt, his sister was "the most hunted person of the modern age." He promised to help her sons. The mourners applauded.

DIANA, PRINCESS OF WALES

After the service, her coffin was driven 75 miles so her body could be laid to rest at Althorp, on a tiny island where Diana and her brother once played.

Immediately after the funeral, the royal family set up the Diana, Princess of Wales, Memorial Fund. Elton John donated the proceeds from "Candle '97" to the memorial fund. Contributions in the millions ensure aid for Diana's charities.

Diana, Princess of Wales, inspired as many theories as books about her. Millions of words have analyzed what she thought and how she felt during her 36 years. But in the end, what matters is what she did.

She reached through the dark tunnel of her own private fears. She warmed a country chilled by its own monarchy. She provided heirs for its throne. Her celebrity status encircled the disadvantaged, raising millions of dollars for their causes. Her sympathetic smile embraced the pain of the ill, the maimed, and the suffering. In the process, she touched us all.

Further Reading

Brennan, Kristine. *Diana, Princess of Wales*. Philadelphia: Chelsea House Publishers, 1999.

Campbell, Lady Colin. *The Princess Nobody Knows*. New York: St. Martin's Press, 1992.

Dempster, Nigel, and Peter Evans. *Behind Palace Doors: Marriage and Divorce in the House of Windsor*. New York: G.P. Putnam's Sons, 1993.

Martin, Ralph G. *Charles and Diana*. New York: G.P. Putnam's Sons, 1985.

Morton, Andrew. *Diana: Her True Story—In Her Own Words*. New York: Simon and Schuster, 1997.

Smith, Sally Bedell. *Diana in Search of Herself*. New York: Random House, 1999.

Chronology

1961	Born at Park House, Norfolk, England, on July 1.
1967	Mother leaves father.
1969	Parents' divorce is finalized; father wins custody of children.
1970–73	Attends Riddlesworth Hall; earns Legett Cup for helpfulness.
1973–77	Attends West Heath; earns Miss Clark Lawrence Award for service.
1975	Inherits title of Lady Diana Spencer after death of seventh Earl Spencer.
1977	Father marries Raine McCorquodale; Diana meets Prince Charles in November.
1978–81	Lives in London, working part-time jobs.
1981	Prince Charles proposes on February 6; engagement announced on February 24; marries Prince Charles on July 29; first official tour as Princess of Wales to principality of Wales in October.
1982	Prince William Arthur Philip Louis ("Wills") born on June 21.
1983	Tours Australia in March, returns as Diana the superstar.
1984	Prince Henry Charles Albert David ("Harry") born on September 15.
1992	Andrew Morton's biography *Diana: Her True Story* published in June; "Squidgy tapes" between James Gilbey and Diana revealed on August 25; officially separates from Prince Charles on December 9.
1993	Temporarily retires from public life on December 3.
1994	During television interview on June 29, Charles admits adultery.
1995	During television interview on November 20, Diana admits adultery.
1996	Divorces Prince Charles on August 28.
1997	Embraces land-mine issue and tours Angola in January; donates dresses for charity auction on June 25; publicizes land-mine issue in Bosnia on August 8; dies in Paris car crash on August 31; buried at Althorp estate on September 6.

INDEX